When Rivers Burned:

The Earth Day Story

by Linda Crotta Brennan

Illustrations by Lisa Greenleaf

I dedicate this book to my husband Robert,
my genial companion in the wilderness. ~LCB

To Sheriff Bob and my MTLO, who help keep
me calm throughout my sea of projects. ~LG

Apprentice Shop Books, LLC
Amherst, New Hampshire

Text copyright ©2013

For information regarding permissions contact:
Apprentice Shop Books, LLC
Box 375
Amherst, NH 03031
www.apprenticeshopbooks.com

LIBRARY OF CONGRESS CATALOGING-IN-PUBLICATION DATA

Crotta Brennan, Linda
    When Rivers Burned: The Earth Day Story by Linda Crotta Brennan; Illustrations by Lisa Greenleaf
    p.cm. – Once, in America Series
    Includes glossary and index
    1. Earth Day—History—the 1970s—juvenile literature.

ISBN-13: 978-0-9842549-9-6
ISBN-10: 0-9842549-9-4

Printed in United States of America

Cover design, illustrations, and book design by Lisa Greenleaf
Greenleaf Design Studio www.Lisagreenleaf.com

Table Contents:

Once, in America. . .

citizens were sickened by smog; pesticides wiped
out wildlife in towns, fields, and forests;
and the rivers were dirty enough to burn.

Chapter 1:
Trouble in Paradise

Silent Spring

Man against insect, it was an age-old conflict. Insects devoured man's crops and spread devastating disease. The few weapons humans had were chemicals that were also poisonous to people, like **lead arsenate**, or substances that were hard to get, like the **pyrethrum** which came from a flower grown mainly in Africa.

During most wars, more men were killed by disease than by the enemy. Bedbugs and lice spread **typhus**, mosquitoes carried **malaria**, and house flies spread **dysentery** through the troops. But for World War II, people had a new weapon. A Swiss chemist, Dr. Paul Hermann

Muller, had developed an insecticide that killed insects on contact, and was apparently safe for humans. This wonder-chemical was **DDT**.

When the Americans captured Naples, Italy in 1943, the city overflowed with refugees. Many were crawling with lice. A major typhus epidemic was about to explode. It was the perfect opportunity to try out the new insecticide. The American general ordered everyone to be dusted with DDT. It stopped the typhus cold.

Soon all Allied troops carried cans of DDT powder to protect against disease-bearing insects. Dr. Muller was awarded the Nobel Prize in 1948 for his part in saving so many lives.

Spraying DDT to kill mosquitoes. No one thought spraying the chemical would harm people.

The Wire Mill, Donora, PA

When World War II was over, chemical companies had stockpiles of DDT. They converted the surplus in order to sell their product for civilian use. One ad proclaimed, *Exactly as used by the U.S. Armed Forces, Insect-O-Blitz, Doom to Insects, Boom to Sales*. Soon airplanes were dropping DDT on croplands and forests. Trucks wove through suburban streets spraying children at play. Housewives even bombed their homes with DDT.

The editor of all U.S. Fish and Wildlife Service publications, Rachel Carson, began to see some disturbing research come across her desk. Apparently, DDT wasn't as harmless as the chemical companies led people to believe.

Killer Smog

Folks in Donora, Pennsylvania were proud of their pollution. Their town had such a huge concentration of factories that it burned as much coal in a day as the large city of Pittsburgh.

"People came to Donora because smoke meant jobs," Donora native, Dr. Devra Lee Davis, remembered. People would ask about the smoke's funny smell. Her grandfather would answer, "That smells like money." On summer evenings, Dr. Davis' family would sit on lawn chairs to watch the fiery spray from smokestacks lighting up the sky like giant sparklers.

Dynamics of a Temperature Inversion

Usually the air closest to the ground is warmer than the air high in the atmosphere. That's because air cools as it rises. Since cool air is heavier than warm air, the cooled air high in the atmosphere sinks, circulating and mixing the air.

A temperature inversion occurs when a layer of high warm air caps an area, preventing the air from circulating. Pollutants are trapped under the cap and can build up to dangerous levels.

But on October 26, 1948, a cap of cold, still air settled above the town, trapping that money scented smoke in Donora's narrow valley. The smoke was a mix of sulfur, carbon monoxide, and heavy metal dust from Donora's many factories, plus poisonous **fluoride gas** spewed from the Donora Zinc Works. The smoke grew so thick that you couldn't see your hand at the end of your arm.

Santa Barbara Oil Spill

In 1966, President Lyndon Baines Johnson needed money to fund the increasingly expensive

The Santa Barbara oil spill occurred on January 28, 1969.

Vietnam War. He offered U.S. oil rights off the shore of California to the highest bidders.

Union Oil was granted a lease to drill near Santa Barbara. The well, Platform Alpha, would bore deep below the ocean floor. To prevent oil and gas from escaping, federal regulations required casing around the entire length of a well's shaft to protect against a rupture. But Union Oil got permission to build casing along only the first couple hundred feet of the shaft.

Dr. Paul Ehrlich studied the Checkerspot Butterfly. It became endangered as pollution filled the air, climate changed, and buildings and other species took over its habitat.

On Tuesday morning, January 28, 1969, workers were trying to replace a drill bit when there was a natural gas blowout. They managed to cap it, but this only built up the pressure inside the well. The meager casing wasn't able to withstand the strain, and a fragile east-west **fault** along the ocean floor fractured in five places, spewing natural gas and crude oil.

At first Union Oil tried to hush things up. Then an anonymous caller dialed Bob Sollen, a reporter with the Santa Barbara News. "The ocean is boiling around Platform A," a male voice said. "Thousands of tons of oil are headed for the beach."

Population Bomb

It all began with butterflies. Dr. Paul Ehrlich was an **entomologist**, an insect scientist. He studied things such as the development of DDT resistance in fruit flies. But his specialty was butterflies. When he became a professor at Stanford University, he researched how Checkerspot Butterfly populations were affected by restrictions on their food, plants and other resources.

Dr. Ehrlich and his wife Anne took a trip around the world to study the **ecology** of butterflies on a global level. As they traveled through Europe, Africa, India, Asia, and the South Pacific, they saw people trying to scratch a living from overcrowded and barren landscapes.

Dr. Ehrlich applied what he'd learned from studying insects to studying humans. "It's the same system," Dr. Ehrlich explained. "We're all

The pollution on the Cuyahoga River burned many times. This picture shows a burn in 1953.

subject to exactly the same laws." He concluded that human numbers were so high, that we had exhausted our natural resources. The people's life-support systems—their food, their water, their soil, their air—were all used up and worn out.

A River on Fire

Sunday, June 22, 1969 was a quiet day in Cleveland, Ohio. Temperatures were in the eighties. There was little wind. As the Cuyahoga River bubbled and broiled through the center of the city, floating oil and garbage piled up around the base of a railway bridge. A train chugged across,

pulling an open car from the steel mill. A blob of molten steel splashed out and landed on the river. That was all it took.

The stew of oil, chemicals, and garbage floating on the river ignited. Flames shot up. The wooden trestles of the bridge caught fire. Firemen and fireboats responded quickly and within half an hour the fire was out.

At the Cleveland Bureau of *NBC News*, they heard the police scanner broadcast about the fire. Reporter Joe Mosbrook called the fire department. They told him that the bridge was shut down and the steel mill would be closed for a few days. There was about $50,000 worth of damage, but nobody was hurt. "It was a relatively minor story," Mosbrook said.

It wasn't the first time the Cuyahoga caught on fire. The river had burned about a dozen times since 1868. It wasn't the river's worst fire, either. In the 1930s the river blazed for two straight days. Back in 1952, a welder's spark ignited oil on the river that burned waterfront property and six

Gaylord Nelson grew up in a pristine area of Wisconsin.

tugboats, causing over a million dollars in damage.

And the Cuyahoga wasn't the only industrial waterway to catch fire. The Schuylkill River in Philadelphia, the Arthur Kill in New York City, the Chicago River, and Baltimore Harbor had all burned.

Vast areas of our country were blighted by smog, pesticides, population pressure, and water pollution, but a boy named Gaylord Nelson had grown up in pristine wilderness.

Chapter 2: A Boy Named Happy

Gaylord Nelson grew up loving the outdoors.

A Love of Nature

Gaylord Nelson was born on January 4, 1916 in the small town of Clear Lake, in the northwestern corner of Wisconsin. The surrounding area was dotted by glacial lakes. Forests stretched north to Lake Superior. Only 700 people lived in Gaylord's small town.

Each fall, Gaylord Nelson watched turtles set off on a migration march down Main Street. They were leaving their summer home in Clear Lake on one end of town to hibernate in the soft bottom of Mud Lake on the other. It fascinated Gaylord that even if he picked a turtle up and set it down facing the wrong direction, it would quickly turn around and head unerringly back toward Mud Lake.

Gaylord was Nelson's given name, but his nickname through elementary school and high school was "Happy." And that's what he was. The outdoors was his playground. He grew up camping, hiking, and hunting. He had every imaginable pet, from dogs and pigeons to snakes, skunks, and even a great horned owl.

Gaylord Nelson enlisted in the Army during World War II.

Progressive Party

Theodore Roosevelt had been a Republican, but his poor opinion of Republican President Taft forced Roosevelt to break away. He formed the Progressive Party in 1912. The party supported liberal issues such as labor reforms, women's suffrage, an end to child labor, and the regulation of industry. The party remained a force in politics until 1952.

Gaylord Nelson's dad was a doctor, and Gaylord thought he'd be a doctor, too. But when he was ten years old, his father took him to hear a speech by Senator Robert La Follette Jr., member of the **Progressive Party**. Gaylord was quite taken with him.

"Do you think you might like to go into politics?" Gaylord's father asked on the ride home.

"I would," Gaylord admitted. "But I'm afraid Bob La Follette may not have left any problems for me to solve."

Young Gaylord was intelligent, but he rarely bothered to study. He tried and quit college twice before settling in at San Jose State College in California. After he finally got his bachelor's degree, he went on to the University of Wisconsin where he studied law.

Nelson graduated in 1942. The Japanese had bombed Pearl Harbor the December before, and the United States plunged into World War II. Nelson enlisted in the army. He was assigned to be one of the white officers over an all-black company.

His men had the worst barracks on base, tar paper shacks where the coal fired stoves threw off so much soot that Nelson said, "You'd wake up

Carrie Lee Dotson, the U.S. Army nurse Gaylord met in Japan, became his wife in 1947.

with your profile on your pillow." Nelson and his troops weren't just plagued by inner air pollution. Prejudice was rampant, too. Nelson said, "I felt the discrimination myself, because you identify with your troops."

Later, he was reassigned to Japan where Nelson began dating an army nurse named Carrie Lee Dotson. After the war was over, Carrie returned to her home in Richmond, VA. Nelson went back to Clear Lake and got involved in politics, but the two stayed in touch.

Eventually, Nelson convinced Carrie Lee to take a new job as a nurse in the hospital at the University of Wisconsin. One night, he took her for a romantic stroll across campus. Walking along the lake, he stopped, shifted from foot to foot, and finally pulled out a diamond ring. "Here," he said, "my mother wanted me to give this to you." Gaylord and Carrie were married November 15, 1947 and settled in Madison, the capital of Wisconsin, where Gaylord had joined a law practice.

Gaylord Nelson (left) campaigns for governor.

Nelson leaving the voting booth.

Nelson ran for Wisconsin state senator in 1948. He was one of the first Democratic senators to be elected in Wisconsin, which was a very Republican state. Remembering his days as officer of an all-black company, one of the first pieces of legislation Nelson introduced was a bill to integrate the Wisconsin National Guard.

At the Democratic Wisconsin State Convention in 1958, Nelson's party chose him as their candidate for governor. It was a bittersweet event. That night, Gaylord's father had a stroke. When Gaylord went to the hospital, his dad asked with a chuckle, "Well, do you think Bob La Follette left enough problems for you?" Two weeks later, his father was dead.

As he campaigned around the state, Gaylord Nelson's folksy stories about Clear Lake characters warmed up the crowds. It was hard not to like him. Still, he expected to lose, since Democrats were such a minority in Wisconsin. But on election night, Nelson watched with elation as the results rolled in. He had won a stunning victory.

Oil spills, water pollution, and the use of DDT devastated insect and animal life.

Chapter 3: Early Battles Against Pollution

Poison in the Air

Mrs. Crow was a student when the Donora smog hit. She remembered, "Dad couldn't drive us to school because it was so hard to see. He had to walk us there that Wednesday with a flashlight, which we thought was fun." But things turned tragic the next day when her grandmother died. "They tried to blame it on asthma," Mrs. Crow said, "But we knew that wasn't true. She was always so strong. It was that smog from the mills."

Frantic calls flooded the Donora emergency line. Firefighters toted oxygen tanks up and down the streets to people struggling to breathe. The firefighters had to feel their way along the buildings, going up to the houses and straining to see their numbers.

Area hospitals overflowed with patients suffering from abdominal cramps, headaches, nausea, and vomiting. So many people died that the community center was forced to serve as a morgue.

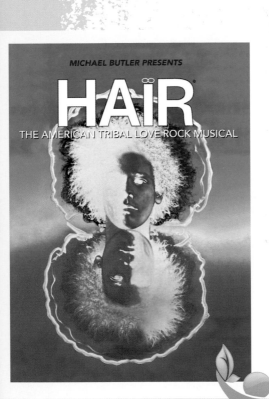

MICHAEL BUTLER PRESENTS

HAIR

THE AMERICAN TRIBAL LOVE ROCK MUSICAL

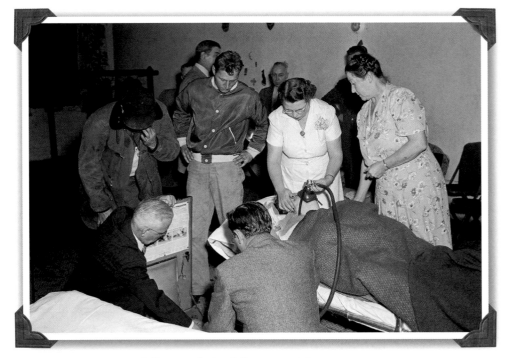

A Donora volunteer helps a smog victim use oxygen.

"Air"

The musical, *Hair*, written by Jim Rado, Gerry Ragni, and Galt MacDermot, opened off-Broadway in 1967. One of its songs, "Air," ended like this:

Welcome sulfur dioxide,
Hello carbon monoxide
The air, the air is everywhere
Breathe deep, while you sleep,
breathe deep

The president of Donora's Health Board asked the Zinc Works to shut down. They refused. Finally, at 6 a.m. Sunday morning, the Zinc Works relented and closed. That afternoon, rains came and washed the smog away. The Zinc Works reopened the next Monday morning.

By then 6,000 were sickened and 20 people were dead. More died in the weeks that followed.

Donora Zinc Works said that they weren't to blame for the event, claiming that it was an "act of God." However, they did pay **settlement money** to families affected by the tragedy.

The state of Pennsylvania passed a Clean Air Act in 1955, the first state to do so. In 1956, Donora Zinc Works closed its factory and moved elsewhere, leaving thousands out of work.

Smog events in both New York City (left) and London (above) killed thousands of people.

Donora wasn't the only place to experience a deadly smog. In 1952 in London, England, over 4,000 people died in a smog so thick that cars were abandoned by the roadside. In the following months, over 8,000 more deaths were attributed to this incident. In New York City, smog events in 1953, 1963, 1965, and 1966 killed hundreds of people. In Los Angeles, with its eye-burning, choking air, the death rate soared whenever smog levels were high.

Chapter 3: Early Battles Against Pollution

Rachel Carson was a Fish and Wildlife biologist when she became concerned about the effects of DDT on plant and animal life.

Silent Spring

While some citizens suffered from the effects of poisoned air, others noticed the damage caused on plant and animal life by chemical sprays.

At her job with Fish and Wildlife, Rachel Carson became more and more concerned about the effects of DDT on the environment. She was a biologist, but she was also a talented writer. In 1945, she wrote to *Reader's Digest*, proposing an article on DDT. The magazine rejected the idea.

So Carson went on to other writing projects. One was a book about the ocean called *The Sea Around Us*. Readers loved its lyrical description of the ocean and its inhabitants. The book became a bestseller. Its success allowed Carson to quit her job and write full time.

Then a letter from a friend reawakened Carson's interest in pesticides. The friend owned a private bird sanctuary. She was horrified by the devastation to wildlife caused by DDT sprayed near her home.

Carson began to investigate. She discovered that DDT had far-reaching effects. It killed beneficial insects like the bees needed to pollinate crops. It killed livestock in treated fields. It created massive fish die-offs. And birds eating DDT-laced worms died in convulsions, even a year after an area was sprayed.

Insect pests soon developed a resistance to DDT. So manufacturers were driven to develop more potent, and poisonous, chemicals.

The trouble was, DDT and similar pesticides didn't break down. They stayed in the environment for years. Animals ate plants and insects treated with pesticides. The pesticides entered the animals' bodies. Then, they passed the chemicals on to the creatures that ate them. The chemicals worked their way up the food chain, accumulating in ever higher doses in animal tissues. And in human tissues. Scientists had discovered DDT in people all over the world, even in the Arctic. No one knew what the long-term effect would be on human health.

After years of careful research, Rachel Carson finally published her book on pesticides, *Silent Spring*, in 1962. Written with grace and power, the book soared to number one on the *New York Times* bestseller list. It began,

---

There was once a town in the heart of America where all life seemed to live in harmony with its surroundings…Then a strange blight crept over the area…new kinds of sickness appeared…There was a strange silence…The birds… where had they gone? Hens brooded, but no chicks hatched…The farmers were unable to raise any pigs. Apple trees were coming into bloom, but no bees droned among the blossoms….

The chemical companies launched a quarter-million-dollar attack. Dr. Robert White-Stevens, spokesman for the chemical industry, maintained

Rachel Carson is pictured holding Silent Spring.

that, "The major claims in Miss Rachel Carson's book, *Silent Spring*, are gross distortions of the actual facts… Miss Carson believes the balance of nature is a major force in the survival of man, whereas the modern scientist believes man is controlling nature."

President John F. Kennedy asked his Science Advisory Committee to investigate the book's claims. Though Rachel Carson was dying of breast cancer, she appeared before the committee to answer questions. She had over fifty pages of meticulously documented sources. The investigation upheld her findings.

Chapter 4: The Push for Change

Gaylord Nelson is sworn in as senator by Vice-president Lyndon Johnson in 1963.

Adding Quality

The GNP or **Gross National Product** is a measurement of all the goods and services produced by a nation. It is used to determine how well a nation is doing. Senator Nelson argued that the GNP should not be the only yardstick of America's well-being. The state of its environment and the happiness of its people were important too. Senator Nelson said the U.S. needed to put "Gross National Quality on par with Gross National Product."

Protecting the Environment

Conserving the environment was Gaylord Nelson's major concern. As governor of Wisconsin, he fought for more rights for minorities and women, better health care for the elderly, and improved education. But he never forgot his rural, small town roots. The environment was his top priority. He pushed through legislation that made Wisconsin a pioneer in environmental protection. He also began a state-funded program to buy private lands to preserve as wilderness areas.

But by 1962, Nelson felt he had achieved everything he could as governor of Wisconsin. He didn't believe that the states had enough power to protect the environment. Local politicians were too easily swayed by the promise of jobs from big corporations. The environment was an issue that needed to be handled at the national level. Nelson set his sights on Washington, running for U.S. senator.

Nelson won the election and was sworn in as senator in 1963. In an interview, he said, "I think the most crucial domestic issue facing America… is the conservation of our natural resources."

In a memo to President Kennedy, Nelson argued that the time was right to focus on environmental issues.

Henry David Thoreau was an American philosopher, naturalist, and writer. His most famous book was *Walden* about a year he spent living alone in a rustic cabin close to nature.

Aldo Leopold was the father of wildlife ecology. A scientist, teacher, and philosopher, he wrote *A Sand County Almanac* about his observations of nature from his summer shack in Wisconsin.

But he soon discovered that only a small fraction of congressmen cared about conservation issues. He set about trying to change that.

Only two weeks after his election as senator, Nelson convinced Robert Kennedy that his brother, President John Kennedy, should make a conservation tour. It would be good politics, Nelson argued in a memo to the president. Interest in the environment was widespread. It included everyone from ladies who planted flowers in window boxes to hunters with high powered rifles. Nelson was convinced that people were ready to move on the issue. They simply needed a leader.

So a trip was planned for President Kennedy to visit eleven states in five days. Nelson prepared nine pages of references and quotes from environmental writers such as Henry David Thoreau, Aldo Leopold, and Rachel Carson for President Kennedy to use in his speeches.

But the day Nelson and the President left for the conservation tour, the U.S. Senate voted to ratify a **nuclear test ban treaty**. That was all the news reporters wanted to talk about. "Every place we went," Nelson said, "the press peppered the

The Nuclear Test Ban Treaty

After eight years of negotiation, the United States, United Kingdom, and the Soviet Union signed a Nuclear Test Ban Treaty on August 5, 1963. The treaty pledged that these nations would stop all nuclear tests and explosions under water, in the atmosphere, or in outer space. They were still allowed to test nuclear weapons underground, as long as all radioactive debris fell within that nation's boundaries. These three countries also pledged to end the nuclear arms race and work toward total nuclear disarmament.

Nelson successfully passed a bill to protect the Appalachian Trail.

president with questions about foreign policy. They didn't really care what he had to say about the environment." The tour was a bust.

Back in Washington, civil rights, the Vietnam War, and nuclear disarmament all clamored for attention. Nelson's conservation issues were pushed aside. But he continued to promote them in the senate, one slow step at a time. He fought to ban synthetic detergents that polluted waterways, and lost. He introduced a bill to protect the **Appalachian Trail** and establish other trails like it. It passed. He made some headway in trying

to pass legislation regulating DDT. Meanwhile, Nelson practiced the give and take of politics, befriending both Democrats and Republicans.

Still, he stood by his principles. In 1965, he was one of only three senators to vote against an increase in money for the Vietnam War. When asked about it, he told the reporter, "I need my conscience more than the president needs my vote."

As he gained experience as a senator, Nelson kept looking for a way to push environmental issues to the forefront of the political agenda.

Chapter 5: Fragile Earth

Dr. Paul Ehrlich

Population Bomb

In 1966, Dr. Paul Ehrlich and his wife Anne returned from their world tour. Dr. Ehrlich was a butterfly expert, but he'd also made significant observations of human populations. He began to give lectures about human ecology.

He told his listeners that the world was facing disaster. The human population was growing beyond the ability of the earth to provide for it. In the years ahead, the planet would get more and more crowded. Food would become scarce. The environment would be destroyed.

Overcrowding would force people to use up the earth's resources to survive. The land would be stripped of its forests and mineral resources. The soil would wear out. Animals would become extinct.

The population was growing fastest in poor countries. Yet the wealthier nations harmed the environment more. They consumed much more than their share of the earth's resources. The United States was a bigger threat than the masses of people in China and India.

Some of his speeches were broadcast on radio and television. The executive director of the conservation organization, Sierra Club saw Dr. Ehrlich on TV and contacted him, urging him to write a book. "Too busy," Ehrlich replied. "I'm flattered by the suggestion, but I really don't have time."

But eventually Dr. Ehrlich was persuaded to give it a try. He and his wife got to work. Anne and Paul wrote the book together, but their editor insisted that only Paul's name appear on the cover.

Their book, *The Population Bomb*, was published in 1968. It claimed that all environmental problems had one source; "All can be traced easily to too many people." The earth had limited resources which were already strained to the breaking point. "The battle to feed all of humanity is over. In the 1970s and 1980s hundreds of millions of people will starve to death in spite of any crash program embarked upon now."

The Ehrlichs argued that if people didn't find a "birth rate solution," human population would eventually be controlled by the "death rate solutions" of war, disease, and famine.

They felt that voluntary birth control would never work. Instead they urged that governments enforce birth control as "coercion in a good cause." In *The Population Bomb*, they suggested that

Dr. Paul Ehrlich's insect studies led him to believe that the human population was also threatened.

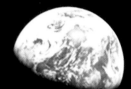

Photo of Earth from Space

In December 1968, Astronaut Bill Anders snapped a photograph of earth from space. It would be become one of the most widely reproduced photographs in history. It made people realize that earth was small, precious, and fragile.

Chapter 5: Fragile Earth

adding sterilization drugs to the water supply in the United States might work, although appropriate drugs didn't exist yet. They also felt all women should have access to safe abortions. The book emphasized the importance of family planning in poor areas such as India and South America. And it criticized the stance of the Catholic Church on birth control.

Many people condemned these positions. Reporter Charles McCabe wrote fourteen columns attacking Ehrlich, saying he was "worse than Hitler."

Biologist Barry Commoner accused Ehrlich of being "anti-poor." A few years later, their long-running dispute came to a head at a United Nations environmental conference. Paul Ehrlich was on stage, trying to give a speech. Commoner wove through the seats in the balcony, passing out notes and questions and egging on his followers. They harassed Paul Ehrlich as his wife, Anne, cringed in the audience. Paul finally stopped and cried, "Come on out, Barry baby!" But Commoner never showed his face.

Controversy drew big audiences. Dr. Ehrlich often appeared on Johnny Carson's "The Tonight Show" and on "NBC News." "Anne is the brains," Paul Ehrlich said, "I'm the mouth." Dr. Ehrlich was abrasive and outspoken, making comments like, "the one thing we'll never run out of is imbeciles."

The Population Bomb sold over three million copies. Dr. Ehrlich's contentious views brought him into conflict with everyone from political commentators to religious leaders. His dire claims earned him the nickname, "Dr. Doom." But his book opened people's eyes to the limits of earth's resources.

Chapter 6:
A Drive for Purpose

Denis Hayes

Denis Hayes grew up in Camas, Washington. The town was nestled in the Columbia River Valley, surrounded by the majestic peaks of Mount Saint Helens, Mount Adam, and Mount Hood. Hayes described it as "some of the most beautiful country on earth."

But Camas was a **mill town**. Its citizens, including Hayes' father, either worked for the paper mill, or provided services for the people who did. The paper mill would **clear cut** the surrounding forests. It poured huge amounts of toxic sludge into the Columbia River. Its smokestacks spewed hydrogen sulfide and sulfur dioxide. The chemicals'

rotten egg stench gave Camas the reputation of being the smelliest place around.

Hayes was keenly aware that the source of his town's prosperity was destroying its Eden-like beauty. He was sure that there "had to be a better way to…meet the needs of a modern industrial civilization."

For Hayes, the times were troubling. He said, "I grew deeply estranged from a world caught in a nuclear-tipped cold war; a world in which black people in the American south and in South Africa were beaten and killed for seeking even rudimentary rights; in which my nation was fighting on the

Denis Hayes grew up in Camas, Washington a paper mill town on the Columbia River.

Chapter 6: A Drive for Purpose

Denis Hayes spent three years traveling through Africa, the Middle East, Asia, and Soviet Union.

wrong side of a war in Southeast Asia." But as a kid from a small town, Hayes felt powerless to change things.

After two years of college, he left and spent the next two years wandering the world. He wasn't interested in Europe. What he wanted to see were the places that were deeply foreign to Americans: Asia, Africa, the Middle East, and the Soviet Union. He was searching for a way to make sense of our human-dominated planet.

What he saw discouraged him. After a depressing month in South Africa, he wandered north to the small African nation of Namibia.

While in Namibia, Hayes considered how the study of ecology could help mankind.

As he lay alone in the Namibian desert one night, hot, thirsty, and hungry, he began thinking about ecology.

"Prior to then, I would have no more turned to ecology for a source of inspiration for human political activism than I would have turned to chemistry or physics or–[even]–music." But he got to thinking about how ecology applied to human societies. "I'd never heard this sort of thinking from anyone else. I felt it offered me a chance to make an original contribution." He stayed awake all night and arose the next morning with a new sense of purpose.

Denis Hayes returned from the desert in Namibia and enrolled in Stanford University. He was elected student body president. He also became involved in protests against the Vietnam War, helping lead 1,000 students in a take-over of Stanford's weapons' research lab.

College students all over the country protested America's participation in the Vietnam War.

Denis had traveled the world. He'd studied and been elected a leader. He'd learned to organize large groups. All of these experiences would come in handy. Within a year of leaving Stanford, Denis Hayes would face an even bigger challenge. He was ready.

Chapter 7:
Sullied Waters

Mayor Carl Stokes

Burning Rivers

The burning Cuyahoga had one important ally, Carl Stokes. He was Cleveland's new mayor. New black mayor.

Carl Stokes recognized the connection between environmental issues and social issues. By the mid-nineteen sixties, America's inner cities were decaying. Their air was foul with smog and garbage blew through the streets. The white middle class had fled to the suburbs, leaving an increasingly poor, powerless, and angry population behind.

Carl Stokes was determined to turn things around. He had already convinced the people of Cleveland to fund a million dollar upgrade for the city's aging sewage system. But he realized Cleveland didn't have the power to clean up all the Cuyahoga's problems on its own. He seized the opportunity of the Cuyahoga fire to spotlight the problems of industrial pollution.

As the first African-American mayor of a major American city, the nation's eyes were upon him. So when Carl Stokes headed down to the Cuyahoga the Monday after the fire to declare a war on water pollution, national reporters went

The Cuyahoga River in 1970. This picture of trash and dead fish was taken behind a popular restaurant called Pickle Bill's.

Workers clean a beach near Santa Barbara.

Journalist Richard Ellers showed the extent of the pollution when he dipped his hand in the Cuyahoga River.

with him. What they found was a stinking, bubbling cauldron of raw sewage, acids, chemicals, oil, animal parts, and debris. One reporter, Richard Ellers, dipped his hand into the river. It came out coated with an oozing, gooey black glove.

For years, steel mills, paint companies, oil companies, chemical companies, the slaughterhouse, and ordinary people had dumped their wastes in the river. And it was all perfectly legal. There was no law against it.

The story of the Cuyahoga fire ran on television and in *Time Magazine*. *Time's* story said, "Some River! Chocolate-brown, oily, bubbling with subsurface gases, it oozes rather than flows."

The picture *Time* ran with its article wasn't from the 1969 fire. It was a more dramatic shot from the 1952 fire, but that didn't matter. The photograph became a symbol that inflamed American's passions. How could a river catch on fire? Something was terribly wrong.

Santa Barbara Oil Spill

When they learned of the oil spill, the people of Santa Barbara rallied. College students, shopkeepers, surfers, parents, and kids joined in the beach cleanup. Men tossed hay on the water to soak up the oil. Others raked it up and loaded it into truck beds to cart it away.

A well-to-do woman ferried oil-soaked seabirds in the backseat of her Mercedes to the rescue station hastily set up at the Santa Barbara Zoo. Their volunteers carefully cleaned the birds'

Despite the efforts of Santa Barbara volunteers, two thirds of the wildlife affected by the oil spill died.

feathers. Despite their efforts, less than a third of the birds survived.

Naturalist John McKinney wrote about wandering the shore pulling birds, alive and dead, out of the gunk. "The oil covers my hands, sticks to my sneakers, spatters my shirt and pants. But it isn't so much the feel of it as the sight and smell of it." It was like "hell before the Devil lit a match."

Union Oil workers struggled for eleven days before the spill was contained. By then a black tide six inches thick covered eight-hundred square miles of ocean and thirty-five miles of coast.

As camera crews congregated to cover the disaster, visions of dying dolphins, poisoned seals, and birds dripping tar flashed across American's new color television screens.

"I don't like to call it a disaster," said Fred L. Hartley, President of Union Oil, "because there has been no loss of human life. I am amazed at the publicity for the loss of a few birds."

Protestors on the beach booed him. Demonstrators grilled their gas credit cards on barbecue skewers. The people of Santa Barbara joined together in a new organization called GOO. Get the Oil Out!

Killer smog, poisonous pesticides, doomsday predictions of overpopulation, devastating oil spills, burning rivers; people all over the country were worried about the environment. No one in Washington seemed to care. But Gaylord Nelson, flying west to speak about the Santa Barbara Oil Spill, would soon change that.

Chapter 8:
The Big Idea

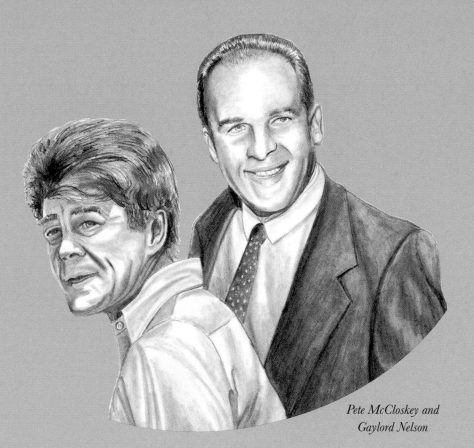

*Pete McCloskey and
Gaylord Nelson*

Gaylord Nelson

In the summer of 1969, Gaylord was invited to speak at a water quality conference in Santa Barbara, California. He saw firsthand the devastation from the recent oil spill. The next day, Nelson flew off to give another speech in Berkeley, California.

During the plane ride, he flipped through a magazine to pass the time. One article arrested his attention. It was a full spread about student-led college **teach-ins** on the Vietnam War. "It popped into my head. That's it!" Nelson said. "Why not have an environmental teach-in and get everyone involved?"

As soon as he returned to Washington, D.C., he set to work. He established a non-profit organization, "Environmental Teach-in, Inc.," and got Republican Paul "Pete" McCloskey to be co-chair, so it would be **bipartisan**. He donated all the fees he received for his conservation speeches as seed money.

Then he began to drum up donations. Some came in from people and organizations already dedicated to the environment. The first was from environmental lawyer Larry Rockefeller. The Conservation Foundation gave generously, as well.

Gaylord Nelson announced plans for an environmental teach-in.

But Nelson cast a wider net. He used his past support of labor bills to solicit a substantial amount from the AFL-CIO Union and the United Auto Workers. UAW President Walter Reuther was glad to help. He told his members, "The auto industry is one of the worst culprits [in creating pollution]," and he asked his union workers to join with the government in creating solutions. "Detroit knows how to design clean cars. And anything they can design, [our] guys can build."

Nelson announced his plan for an environmental teach-in to the public in a speech on September 20, 1969, "I am convinced that the same concern the youth...took in changing this nation's priorities on the war in Vietnam and on civil rights can be shown for the problems of the environment." He called for a national teach-in on the "The Crisis of the Environment" to be held the following spring on college campuses across the country.

Nelson needed a date that didn't fall during college exams or spring break, and didn't conflict with the religious holidays of Easter and Passover. He wanted his teach-in to be midweek, so more students would be on campus. So he scheduled it for Wednesday, April 22, 1970.

Shortly after the wire service put out a story about his announcement, calls and letters flooded his office. Initially, two of his staff members

THE GAYLORD NELSON NEWSLETTER

Washington, D.C.

November 1969

Environmental Teach-In Planned

National Effort Set For Spring

The development of comprehensive plans to kick off a national teach-in on the Crisis of the Environment to take place this spring on college campuses across the country will be announced this month by Sen. Gaylord Nelson.

The Wisconsin senator said he has been traveling around the country talking about his teach-in idea and seeking support for the proposal.

By the end of the month, Nelson expects to have a national headquarters on the teach-in set up in Washington with a staff that will be contacting students all across the country.

The teach-in plans call for a day, probably in April, when normal campus activities will be set aside for the university and the local community to get together and discuss the mutually shared environmental problems.

Discussions, Rallies

On that day, special programs designed and planned by the students will take the form of symposiums, convocations, panel discussions or

Apostle Islands Legislation

The Nelson bill to establish Apostle Islands as a part of the national park system passed the Senate in June, and the Senator is hopeful the House will authorize the necessary money to make the proposal a reality by the end of next year.

beyond what I had hoped," Nelson said. "My office has been receiving mail from students and people from all parts of the nation wanting to know how to become involved and how to plan a teach-in."

disaster of years of wanton, indient waste and destruction of natural resources of the cou Nelson argued. "If somethin done soon, there may be left for their children."

Representative Pete McCloskey

tried to answer them all, but the response was more than they could handle. In Nelson's words, "It simply took off like gangbusters." He needed more than two staffers to organize it.

After one of Nelson's speeches about the event, a group of student militants offered to take over. "Not so fast," said Nelson. He didn't want his teach-in to be transformed into a platform for "calling attention to all the ills" of capitalism and the democratic system.

Nelson got a request for a meeting from a grad student who was hoping to hold an environmental teach-in on Harvard's campus. After the meeting, Nelson asked his co-chair, Pete McCloskey, if he knew anything about this college kid. After all, he had earned his bachelor's degree from Stanford, which was in McCloskey's congressional district. McCloskey asked around. The kid got very high recommendations.

His name was Denis Hayes.

Hayes Accepts the Challenge

After graduating, Denis Hayes enrolled in a brand new Masters Program in Public Policy at Harvard Kennedy School. All students in the program were required to participate in a project outside the university. Hayes read an article in the *New York Times* about Senator Gaylord Nelson and his planned environmental teach-in. That sounded interesting, so Hayes arranged a meeting with Senator Nelson. Hayes hoped to organize the teach-in at Harvard, or maybe even at all the colleges in Cambridge.

But Hayes said, "It quickly became clear that the 'organization' at that point was mostly Gaylord...making speeches." Senator Nelson had gotten Republican Pete McCloskey to be his co-chair, and set up a non-profit for his teach-in, but little else.

At their meeting, Nelson suggested that Hayes organize Boston, and Hayes agreed and returned to Harvard. Two weeks later, he got a call. Would he be willing to quit school and organize the United States? Hayes didn't hesitate. "This could be a unique opportunity to get some serious, big-league experience in the field to which I wanted to devote my life."

Hayes accepted.

Within two weeks of volunteering to organize a Teach-in in Boston, Denis Hayes was asked to take over planning for all the states.

Chapter 9: Creating a New World View

Denis Hayes modeled his teach-in plans after the work of non-violent Indian activist, Mahatma Gandhi.

It's About the Environment

Senator Nelson realized that the time was ripe for the environmental movement and he decided that, like civil rights and the anti-war movement, the effort should be led by the young. He trusted Hayes to pull it off.

"Gaylord (Nelson) was a jewel to work with," said Denis Hayes, "because he was a big-picture guy, who was very comfortable delegating. Gaylord kept his ego in check. This is extremely unusual in the Senate…He made no effort to make it all about him; it was about the environment."

The goal was to build a large, diverse event that encompassed the whole country. Size was important in order to gain media attention. If they were successful, Hayes hoped that they would introduce a new set of values into the American mainstream, changing how people thought about things. "It would be the beginning of a revolutionary new world view." Hayes admitted that this was an ambitious undertaking for someone

*Gandhi taught methods of non-violent **civil disobedience.***

who was only twenty-five at the time.

Hayes modeled his efforts on Mahatma Gandhi's non-violent approach. Like Gandhi, Hayes sought to create the biggest, most inclusive, non-violent demonstration ever. It would not consist of one huge event, said Hayes, "but countless thousands of small events in every town, city, village, and crossroads in America." And like Gandhi, Hayes would give people simple things that they could do to help: recycle, avoid polluting detergents, save water, save energy, and eat organic.

Hayes assembled a staff of about thirty-five paid workers. Some would coordinate different regions. Others dealt with elementary and high schools and colleges. Others kept the paperwork flowing or handled finances or legal issues.

They only had about $185,000 to organize the whole national event. Most of the money came from small contributors. They could have had more money to work with, but when Esso Oil Company (now Exxon) handed them a large donation, Hayes and Nelson decided to refuse it.

Mahatma Gandhi

Mahatma Gandhi led a non-violent movement to free India from British control. He and his followers practiced civil disobedience of unjust laws. He urged Indians to boycott British goods and encouraged them to return any honors given to them by the British. Gandhi's hunger strikes drew the world's attention to India's plight and led Britain to grant India its independence on August 15, 1947.

Gaylord Nelson and Denis Hayes refused to accept Earth Day donations from major polluters like oil companies.

Planning Earth Day

Denis Hayes wanted each community to decide what kind of activities they would sponsor. Each town had different problems to deal with. In a television interview Denis said, "...there are, of course, fairly strong distinctions between a place like Berkeley [CA] and a place like Oklahoma City [OK]..."

Some towns held protests. Others sponsored lectures or speeches. New York City closed some streets to car traffic. Towns held sing-alongs, picked up litter, and organized "read-ins."

They didn't want to owe anything to a major polluter.

The budget was really tight. "We each earned $85 a week," Hayes said. This was only about 2/3 of the average salary at the time. Scores of unpaid volunteers also helped.

Hayes needed to find office space. Senator Nelson had been offered an office for the teach-in, free of charge. But Hayes pointed out that using a brand new office in a building owned by one of America's largest corporations would send the wrong message. Their group would be seen as "**establishment**." Senator Nelson agreed, and the group set up in a shoddier space that they had to rent.

Senator Nelson's original vision was for an "environmental teach-in" on college campuses. But Hayes didn't think that would work. He felt they needed a more inclusive focus and a "brand" or catchy name that people would easily recognize.

Julian Koenig, who wrote ads for major corporations for a living, offered to help. He told Hayes to give him a few days. He returned with ideas for full page ads, with possible names for the event, such as "Environmental Day," "Green Day," "E Day," "Ecology Day."

Some of the first Earth Day team members. Left to right: Denis Hayes, Andrew Garling, Arturo Sandoval, Stephen Cotton, Barbara Reid, and Bryce Hamilton.

April 22.
Earth Day.

A disease has infected our country.
It has brought smog to Yosemite,
dumped garbage in the Hudson,
sprayed DDT in our food,
and left our cities in decay.
Its carrier is man.

The weak are already dying. Trees by the Pacific. Fish in our streams and lakes. Birds and crops and sheep. And people.

On April 22 we start to reclaim the environment we have wrecked.

April 22 is the Environmental Teach-In, a day of environmental action.

Hundreds of communities and campuses across the country are already committed.

It is a phenomenon that grows as you read this.

Earth Day is a commitment to make life better, not just bigger and faster. To provide real rather than rhetorical solutions.

It is a day to re-examine the ethic of individual progress at mankind's expense.

It is a day to challenge the corporate and governmental leaders who promise change, but who shortchange the necessary programs.

It is a day for looking beyond tomorrow, April 22 seeks a future worth living.

April 22 seeks a future.

We are working seven days a week to help communities plan for April 22. We have come from Stanford, Harvard, Bucknell, Iowa, Missouri, New Mexico, Michigan and other campuses.

We are a non-profit, tax exempt, educational organization. Our job is to help groups and individuals to organize environmental programs to educate their communities.

Earth Day is being planned and organized at the local level. In each community people are deciding for themselves the issues upon which to focus, and the activities which are most appropriate.

We can help, but initiative must come from each community. We have heard from hundreds of campuses and local communities in all fifty states. Dozens of conservation groups have offered to help. So have the scores of new-breed environmental organizations that are springing up every day.

A national day of environmental education was first proposed by Senator Gaylord Nelson. Later he and Congressman Paul McCloskey suggested April 22. The coordination has been passed on to us, and the idea now has a momentum of its own.

All this takes money. Money to pay our rent, our phones, our mailings, brochures, staff, advertisements.

No list of famous names accompanies this ad to support our plea, though many offered without our asking.

Big names don't save the environment. People do.

Help make April 22 burgeon. For you. For us. For our children.

The Environmental Teach-In, Inc.
Room 200
2000 P Street, N. W.
Washington, D.C. 20036

I enclose $10, $20, $50_____dollars (tax deductible)
How can I help my community?
Name _____
Address _____

A re-creation of an Earth Day advertisement posted in the New York Times *on January 1970.*

Hayes and his staff met for pizza and beer that night and spread the ads on the floor. They unanimously agreed with Koenig's personal favorite, "Earth Day."

They bought a full page ad in the Sunday *New York Times*. "Environmental teach-in disappeared overnight from everyone's memory," said Hayes. From that moment on the event would be called "Earth Day." The ad had a fundraising coupon on the bottom inside a smoke-belching smokestack. The ad paid for itself many times over as Earth Day office's steady stream of mail turned into a gushing torrent.

The mail represented an incredibly diverse group. Hayes and his staff were surprised by how many letters came from stay-at-home moms. These mothers were worried about their children and threats to human health and the planet. There were also letters from neighborhood groups who were dealing with local issues, like pesticide spraying, polluted waterways, nearby oil drilling, or planned superhighways. Other letters voiced concerns that ranged from the Everglades to Alaska, from marine mammals to bald eagles.

These were the days before the internet. There were no personal computers, word processors, or cell phones. Hayes and his staff looked for cost-effective ways to advertise Earth Day in national and local newspapers. Then, when people contacted them, Hayes' staff entered them in a database. This was just a collection of metal **addressograph** plates arranged in trays by zip code. They used them to print address labels for mass mailings.

The group sent out a pamphlet that included a list of options for activities.

Earth Day would be a national action, but each event would be planned locally. Gaylord Nelson claimed that the remarkable thing about Earth Day was that it organized itself.

Meanwhile, Nelson sent a mailing to every governor in the United States, and to two hundred mayors, asking them to issue Earth Day proclamations.

In the two weeks leading up to April 22nd, Senator Nelson traveled the country, speaking to schools, labor unions, and state legislatures. He told them, "People from coast to coast are disgusted and angry at the accelerating destruction of our environment and the quality of life." Nelson appeared on CBS Television's *Face the Nation*. "No administration

June 21, 1970

by the people of Earth
for the people of Earth

EARTH DAY PROCLAMATION

Chapter 9: Creating a New World View

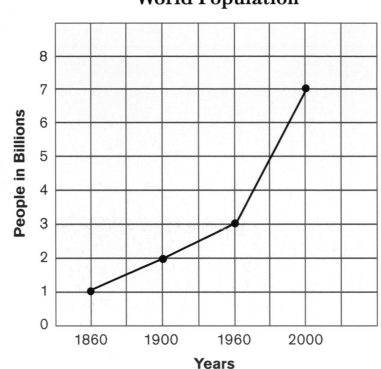

World Population

Gaylord Nelson, like Paul Ehrlich, believed that the population boom had to be addressed in order to solve environmental problems.

has understood the size of the issue," he said. "It is much more important than space, weapons systems, or the money we are wasting in Vietnam." He told audiences that population growth was the world's biggest problem, and if it continued unchecked, "we might as well forget finding solutions to any of our social or environmental problems."

On the eve of Earth Day, Senator Nelson gave a speech at the University of Wisconsin.

"Our goal is an environment of decency, quality, and mutual respect for all human beings and all other living creatures." Nelson told the crowd that the battle to restore the environment would take enormous commitment. "Are we able? Yes. Are we willing? That's the unanswered question."

Meanwhile, Hayes worried. Would Earth Day's big outdoor events get rained out? Would its demonstrations be marred by violence? Would Earth Day be upstaged by other world events?

Chapter 10: Earth Day

April 22, 1970

On the eve of Earth Day, April 21, 1970, Senator Nelson flew home to Madison, Wisconsin, eagerly anticipating his home town's Earth Day parade of nonpolluting vehicles. But the weekend before, a peace rally in Madison had been terrorized by violent radicals breaking windows. Town officials were afraid the radicals might try to disrupt the parade, too. To Nelson's chagrin, they cancelled Madison's celebration.

A small group of people bicycled and marched through Madison anyway, picking up litter along the way. Later that day, Nelson spoke to thousands of students at the University of Wisconsin, telling them of his hope that someday armies might become obsolete and money could be spent on the environment instead of weapons.

On Earth Day itself, Nelson planned to speak at events in Indiana, Colorado, and California.

The First Earth Day, New York City, 1970.

NY Mayor John Lindsay led a parade of bike riders.

NY City was the site of the largest Earth Day demonstration.

Woodstock

In 1969, an estimated 500,000 people gathered for a rock music festival on Yasgur's dairy farm in upstate New York. So many people came that the festival organizers ended up having to throw open the gates and let everyone in for free. Billed as "Three days of Peace and Music," Woodstock became an icon of the **hippie counterculture** movement.

Denis Hayes' Earth Day would begin at the Mall in Washington D.C. with a sunrise ceremony. Then he'd fly on to New York City, Chicago, and back to D.C.

Earth Day, April 22, 1970, dawned bright and sunny in New York City, the site of the biggest demonstration. Republican Mayor John Lindsay closed off Fifth Avenue to traffic. He declared in his Earth Day speech, "We must end this self-poison before it ends us." He walked Fifth Avenue's forty five blocks, leading a parade of people on non-polluting bikes, roller skates, and pogo sticks. Interviewed on national television, Lindsay spoke about how he always picked up litter when he walked, to serve as an example to others. And he promoted mass transit, promising viewers that, "We're building twelve new subway lines in New York City... the city is contributing a billion dollars over the next ten years to mass transit construction...We are discouraging automobile use in the central business areas."

Mike Roche, a participant that day, called Earth Day the "**Woodstock** of the environmentalists."

Mike's wife, Kathy Roche, described the scene. Every kind of person was there, "old people, babies in strollers, black, white, middle class, hippies,

Denis Hayes (left) spoke to millions of people gathered in Central Park in New York City. People created a dance with brooms (above) to mimic cleaning up the Earth.

very traditionally dressed people, Hari Krishna members." There were "booths, floats, parades, street dramas…people doing dances with brooms to clean up the earth, posters with great slogans (and sometimes not such great grammar). A truck brought in clean water from the Catskills for people to taste. Huge sculptural floats made of trash were part of the parade."

"There was a feeling of great optimism," Mike added.

When Denis Hayes arrived, he spoke to over a million people flooding Central Park and spilling out into Fifth Avenue.

Miami, Florida held a "Dead Orange Parade," where the winning float boasted a Statue of Liberty wearing an anti-pollution mask.

At Stanford College in California, Stephanie Mills, a recent grad, pledged never to have children as her contribution to **zero population growth**.

School children took nature hikes, sang anti-pollution songs, and planted trees. One junior high class set up a demonstration of what the world might be like in the future by crowding sixty kids into a classroom filled with smoke.

Things were calmer in Washington, D. C.

Photos from the first Earth Day on April 22, 1970.

Girl Scouts in Washington, D. C. removed litter from the Potomac River.

where girl scouts in canoes pulled junk from the Potomac River. Protesters on the Mall raised a green and white American flag, shouting, "Clean the Earth." They were 10,000 strong by nightfall. They marched to the Department of the Interior, whose leader was away giving an Earth Day speech in Alaska.

In Boston, Earth Day wasn't so peaceful. Demonstrators picketed Logan Airport with signs protesting the development of the SST or Super Sonic Transport, which they feared would create massive air pollution with its emissions and havoc with its sonic booms. They were holding up signs and resting in symbolic coffins when police ordered them to leave, saying they were blocking a public way. The demonstrators started to pack up, but not fast enough for the police, who began shouting and shoving and making arrests.

The SST

NASA and the Air Force had developed "supersonic" planes that went faster than the speed of sound. In the 1960s plans were in the works to create a supersonic transport or SST for civilian use. But when planes accelerate past the speed of sound, they create a sonic boom, powerful enough to break windows on the ground. The engines needed to propel an aircraft into supersonic flight use an enormous amount of fuel and produce massive pollution. U.S funding for the SST was dropped because of these concerns.

Britain and France joined together to create their version of the SST, the Concorde, in 1976. Many countries prohibited the Concorde from flying over their airspace due to its sonic boom. During the oil crisis, the price of fueling the Concorde skyrocketed. The aircraft consistently lost money. The Concorde fleet was permanently grounded in 2003.

*Left to right: Some groups recycled food waste to created garden **mulch**; others did water testing or picked up highway trash.*

Earth Day wasn't just celebrated in major cities, but in practically every town in the United States. Residents of the poor **barrio** in Albuquerque, New Mexico played mariachi music, dressed in folk costumes, and marched to protest the stench of the sewage treatment plant that polluted their water. The people of Omaha, Nebraska collected cans—156,000 of them—and built a tin mountain. Louisianans nominated the oil industry as the "polluter of the month."

While some communities presented "awards" to major polluters, others buried cars and electrical appliances as a protest against the pollution they caused. Townsfolk picked up trash and cleaned rivers. As one kindergartner explained on TV, "We want our city clean." Even people who couldn't take part in a local demonstration showed their support by driving with their lights on during Earth Day.

In the end it was estimated that over 2,000 colleges, 10,000 high schools and elementary schools, and 20,000,000 people took part in that first Earth Day. That equaled a tenth of the population of the United States. It was the largest demonstration in American history.

After it was over, the *New York Times* reported,

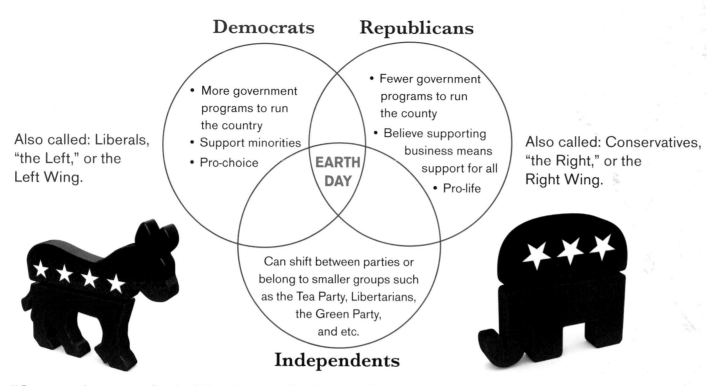

Democrats

- More government programs to run the country
- Support minorities
- Pro-choice

Republicans

- Fewer government programs to run the county
- Believe supporting business means support for all
- Pro-life

EARTH DAY

Also called: Liberals, "the Left," or the Left Wing.

Also called: Conservatives, "the Right," or the Right Wing.

Can shift between parties or belong to smaller groups such as the Tea Party, Libertarians, the Green Party, and etc.

Independents

"Conservatives were for it. Liberals were for it. Democrats, Republicans, and Independents were for it. So were the ins, the outs, the executive and legislative branches of government. It was Earth Day and, like Mother's Day, no man in public office could be against it." Indeed, at the end of the CBS News Earth Day broadcast, President Nixon's spokesman stated that the president had made a full commitment to the environment.

But Earth Day had its critics. The **right-wing**, politically conservative, John Birch Society noted that April 22, 1970 was the Russian Communist leader, Vladimir Lenin's, 100th birthday. They charged that Earth Day was a veiled attempt to honor Lenin. Nelson admitted that the John Birch Society knew more about Lenin's birthday than he did. "On any given day, a lot of both good and bad people were born," he argued. "The world's first environmentalist, Saint Francis of Assisi, was born on April 22. So was Queen Isabella. More importantly, so was my Aunt Tillie."

Others were put off by some of the views presented on Earth Day. During a speech in Milwaukee, Senator Nelson said that the biggest threat to the environment was unchecked population growth. Author Jane Jacobs stood up and challenged him, saying it was only a delusion that population and affluence degraded the environment. The prospect of population control terrified her. "As things stand now, we are not a fit society to possess public powers for population control."

The political left attacked Earth Day, too. They called it a "beautiful snow job" that drew attention away from the important issues of racism, poverty, and the Vietnam War. "We here tonight are being conned," said journalist I. F. Stone. "The country is slipping into a wider war in Southeast Asia and we're sitting here talking about litter bugs."

Walter Cronkite, anchor of CBS News, charged that most participants had a "skylark mood" that contrasted starkly with Earth Day's apocalypse message. "What is at stake," he said, "is survival."

Students at Kent State College held an anti-war demonstration. An Ohio National Guard Jeep is seen in the top center. The soldiers are telling the students to disperse.

So would Earth Day be a one day "frolic in the park" or would it truly make an impact on history?

On April 30, just eight days after Earth Day, President Nixon announced he was escalating the war in Southeast Asia and moving troops into Cambodia.

On May 4, students staged an anti-war protest at Kent State College. The Ohio National Guard fired into the unarmed crowd, killing four students and wounding nine others. The nation erupted. Hundreds of colleges and universities were closed down in protest.

The environment was forgotten.

The National Guard launches tear gas at student protesters.

Chapter 11:
Dirty Dozen

Congressman George Fallon

Congressman E. Ross Adair

Congressman Odin Langen

Congressman Edward Lawrence Winn

Congressman John H. Kyl

Some of the candidates targeted by the Earth Day staff.

Keeping up Momentum

Earth Day had once again been upstaged by world events. It was a replay of how President Kennedy's conservation tour was derailed by the signing of the nuclear test ban treaty. Denis Hayes was as concerned about the Kent State Massacre and the escalation of the Vietnam War as anyone, but he didn't want to see all his hard work raising ecological awareness go down the drain.

He spoke to his Earth Day staff, telling them that they couldn't afford to lose the momentum of an environmental movement that had twenty million people behind it. An election was coming up. "We would be mad not to participate," he said.

But some of his staff believed politics were corrupting. They didn't want to support any particular candidate. So Hayes suggested that they target the candidates with the worst environmental records instead. His staff agreed. One of them came up with a catchy name. They would target a "Dirty Dozen."

Hayes' group searched for candidates who had terrible environmental records, had won their last election by fewer than six percentage points, and were from a district where there was an important environmental issue. They also had to have a strong opponent. The group identified twelve candidates and worked to unseat them.

Mass Transit and Pollution

Automobiles are a major source of air pollution. Mass transit systems, like buses, trains, and trolleys, reduce the use of automobiles and lower air pollution. Mass transit also reduces congestion and makes areas more attractive to walkers and cyclists.

Denis Hayes' committee focused on unseating 12 Congress members who had poor environmental records.

The toughest member of the "Dirty Dozen" was a Democratic congressman from Maryland, George Fallon. He had served in congress for over 25 years and was chairman of the Public Works Committee, which held the purse strings for money allotted for public projects. Fallon was also a major enemy of **mass transit**. Instead he pushed through the Federal Highway Act, the largest amount of money ever authorized for building roads.

On Election Day, due to Denis Hayes' campaign, seven of the twelve "Dirty Dozen" lost their seats, including the powerful George Fallon.

Earth Day's co-chair, Congressman Pete McCloskey, said that the Dirty Dozen campaign scared his colleagues to death. If the environmentalists could take out George Fallon, anyone was vulnerable.

The environment had become a voting issue.

A few weeks after the election, despite heavy lobbying by the coal, oil, auto, steel, and electric industries, the Senate passed a strong new version of the Clean Air Act unanimously. The House of Representatives adopted it by voice vote. This marked the very first piece of legislation sparked by Earth Day.

Then Gaylord Nelson set forth an ambitious environmental agenda in a speech to the senate. "America has bought environmental disaster on

President Richard Nixon signs the Clean Air Act.

History of the Clean Air Act
Congress's first attempt at clean air legislation occurred in 1963. It was passed, with **amendments**, in 1965 (See photo below). The 1970 act expanded those regulations and established the **EPA**.

the installment plan: Buy affluence now, and let future generations pay the price." He called for a new ecological ethic. In practical terms, that meant cleaner auto engines, phosphorus-free detergents, a ban on toxic pesticides, the elimination of non-returnable cans and bottles, anti-pollution devices on jet engines, the creation of a federal environmental advocacy agency, a ban on dumping waste into the oceans and Great Lakes, controls on strip mining, a halt to drilling for oil in the ocean, an environmental education program, a comprehensive national land use policy, public transportation, and more.

He got most of what he asked for. Bowing to the force of public opinion, President Nixon

59

Major Environmental Legislation Passed After the First Earth Day

1970:   Clean Air Act
        Environmental Protection Agency

1971:   Alaska Native Claims Settlement Act

1972:   Clean Water Act
        Coastal Zone Management Act
        Marine Mammal Protection Act
        Marine Protection, Research and Sanctuaries Act

1973:   Endangered Species Act

1974:   Energy Supply and Environmental Coordination Act
        Forest and Rangeland Renewable Resources Planning Act
        Safe Drinking Water Act
        Deepwater Port Act

1975:   Eastern Wilderness Act
        National Environmental Policy Act Amendments

1976:   National Forest Management Act
        Federal Land Policy and Management Act
        Resource Conservation and Recovery Act
        Toxic Substances Control Act
        Federal Coal Leasing Act Amendments

1977:   Clean Water Act Amendments
        Clean Air Act Amendments
        Surface Mining Control and Reclamation Act
        Soil and Water Resources Conservation Act

1978:   Endangered American Wilderness Act
        Outer Continental Shelf Lands Act Amendments
        Omnibus Parks Act

1979:   Archaeological Resources Protection Act

1980:   Comprehensive Environmental Response, Compensation
        and Liability Act (Superfund)

created the Environmental Protection Agency by executive order on December 2, 1970. The EPA's mission would be to establish and enforce environmental protection standards, conduct environmental research, provide help in fighting environmental pollution, and recommend new environmental policies.

In the next eleven years, more environmental legislation was passed than in the nation's entire history. Over 28 major laws were crafted to protect our air, water, food, wild species, and wilderness. These included the Clean Water Act, the Endangered Species Act, and the Federal Environmental Pesticide Control Act, among others.

Chapter 12: A Global Earth Day

To Senator Gaylord Nelson with best wishes, and warm memories of this great day *Bill Clinton*

President Bill Clinton awards Gaylord Nelson the Presidential Medal of Freedom.

End of an Era

Nothing lasts forever. In a Republican political sweep, Democrat Gaylord Nelson lost his bid for reelection in 1980. On January 20, 1981, Ronald Reagan became president, and the **heyday** of environmental legislation came to an end.

Although Nelson was in his mid-sixties by then, he wasn't ready to retire. He went on to become chairman of the Wilderness Society, which had been founded by the writer, Aldo Leopold, one of Nelson's environmental heroes. Nelson acted as the Wilderness Society's spokesman, giving speeches to colleges and organizations across the nation. After twenty years with the Wilderness Society, Nelson asked to be taken off the payroll. But he continued to be active even after that, keeping his office, going to work each day, and traveling to speak about environmental issues, even at age 85. In 1995, on the twenty-fifth anniversary of Earth Day, President Clinton awarded Gaylord Nelson the Presidential Medal of Freedom, the nation's highest civilian honor.

After the first Earth Day, Denis Hayes went back to finish his law degree. He headed President Jimmy Carter's Solar Energy Research Institute from 1983 to 1988. Then Hayes went on to practice private law.

Denis Hayes returned to the Earth Day movement in 1990. This time, the focus was on an international Earth Day.

But in 1990, Hayes left his job at a law firm to head up Earth Day again. This time he took the event international, reaching out to 141 countries. The French created a 500 mile long human chain across the country. There was a trash clean up on the slopes of Mount Everest. The event was a tremendous boost to the recycling movement and was the impetus for the United Nations Earth Summit in Rio de Janeiro in 1992.

Earth Day continued to be celebrated every year, and was expanded into Earth Week. On Earth Day 2000, Gaylord Nelson looked back at all the event had accomplished. "The goal of Earth Day was to inspire a public demonstration so big it would shake the political establishment out of its **lethargy** and force the environmental issue onto the public agenda. That is what happened."

Obvious pollution problems had been cleaned up. Lake Erie's fisheries had been restored. Coastal, wetland, and prairie habitats had been protected. Nelson felt that one of Earth Day's most important legacies was that it sparked a new environmental consciousness in the nation. Earth Day was now celebrated in elementary and high school classrooms across the country. Environmental studies had also been instituted at many colleges and universities.

But Nelson worried that the public was growing **complacent**. They relied on professional environmentalists to watch over the planet. "We are losing the battle," he said. There was much work to

Chapter 12: A Global Earth Day

Fifty years after Rachel Carson wrote Silent Spring, *the sky was once again filled with birds.*

be done on problems such as over-fishing, logging old growth forests, flood plain management, smog, endangered species, and global warming. Nelson felt that the biggest issue, one that fed into everything else, was still overpopulation.

Earth Day still had its detractors. People claimed that environmentalists were "doomsayers" predicting dire consequences that never came to pass. But Denis Hayes argued that, "We look at long term trends and describe where they are headed. Rather frequently, they are quite alarming. Nobody wants to go there, so laws are passed and the fate avoided. Then we are accused of being alarmist."

He went on, "Rachel Carson wrote of a spring without birds. Fifty years later, the skies are full of birds, including most of those she was writing about. But, of course, no one wanted a Silent Spring, so we banned DDT and several other pesticides that were lethal to birds. We [were right about there being a problem], but we fixed it. We did the same thing to air and water pollution, lead in gasoline, CFCs for the ozone layer, etc."

Other critics maintained that environmental

protection costs jobs. Hayes argued that people don't see the whole picture. "Whenever there is economic change, jobs are created and lost." It's just that people see the jobs that are lost, but aren't aware of the jobs that will be gained in the future.

Denis Hayes became president of the Bullitt Foundation, which funded environmental programs in the Pacific Northwest, but he returned to run Earth Day again in 2000. Earth Day participants planted trees, cleaned villages and cities, promoted public transportation, and started recycling and environmental education programs in

places as far-flung as India, Ukraine, Philippines, China, Morocco, Afghanistan, and Paraguay. "In some ways," Hayes said, "we have been much more effective at promoting environmental values in near-destitute developing nations than in some poor neighborhoods in our own [country]." Earth Day organizers also worked with religious organizations, reaching out to over 25,000 congregations.

In 2010, Earth Day was celebrated in over 190 countries by over one billion people, making it the largest civic event in the world.

Today, people all over the world celebrate Earth Day.

Epilogue

New Pest Control Methods

The EPA allows the use of low risk chemical pesticides. Many new biologically based pesticides have been developed, as well. Microbes that infect pests and insects that prey on pests, such as ladybugs and some species of wasps, are also used for pest control.

Silent Spring and DDT

The EPA banned the general use of DDT in the United States on June 14, 1972. Its use was still allowed in special cases, such as to control a disease outbreak. Since then, DDT levels in animal and human tissues have declined. Bird populations have bounced back, especially birds such as the bald eagle, the peregrine falcon, and the brown pelican. In the U.S., there has been no increase in malaria, typhus, or similar insect-spread diseases. Farmers have found other effective ways to control insect pests.

On May 23, 2001, 92 countries signed the Stockholm Convention on Persistent Organic Pollutants or POPs. DDT is one of these POPs, which persist, or don't break down, in the environment. Detractors claim that this ban on DDT claimed millions of lives because of subsequent outbreaks of malaria. Actually, due to improper spraying in developing countries, many malarial mosquitoes had developed a resistance to DDT. The pesticide was no longer effective in killing them. So the increase in malaria cases was caused by DDT resistance, not because they stopped spraying DDT. And DDT is still used when necessary to safeguard human health.

Major Impacts On Air Quality Since Earth Day 1970

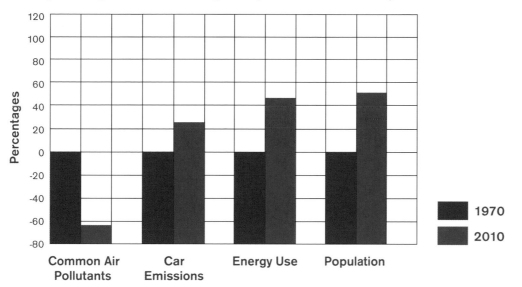

While our population has grown 52%, energy and car use has increased since 1970, air pollution has dropped by 68%.

Donora Smog

In Donora, Pennsylvania, the skies are clear now. Residents are breathing easier. Across the nation, the Clean Air Act has cut down the six major air pollutants by over 50%. It has reduced industrial toxins like those that caused Donora's deaths by over 70%. Cars are 90% more efficient, and the manufacturing of most ozone destroying chemicals has ended. This has been accomplished despite the fact that the U.S. economy has doubled, energy use has gone up by fifty percent, and there are 200% more cars on the road than there were in 1970.

We've made great strides, but the fight to combat air pollution isn't over. The World Health Organization estimates that there are at least three million, and maybe as many as six million, smog-related deaths a year. Part of the problem is the rush of poor nations to industrialize without environmental protection. The world (including the U.S.) is also burning more coal, which is a leading cause of air pollution. "We've come a long way since Donora, but our work is not

Donora, PA now has clean air.

Everlasting Chemicals

In 1995, the United Nations Environment Programme defined Persistent Organic Pollutants or POPs as carbon-based chemicals that remain intact in the environment for many years, become widely distributed in the soil, water, and air due to natural processes, accumulate in the fatty tissues of animals, including humans, concentrating in higher levels up the food chain, and are toxic to both humans and wildlife.

In China, families only are allowed one child.

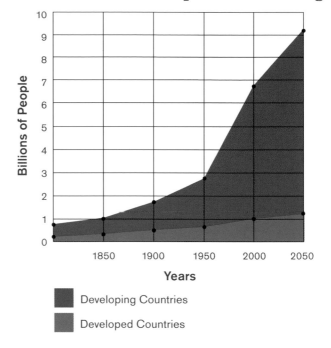

How Is the World's Population Growing?

Developing Countries

Developed Countries

done," says W. Michael McCabe, Donora's local EPA administrator. "America no longer has black skies or belching smokestacks. Today's air quality problems are more insidious…We may never return to the disastrous conditions of Donora, but we need to keep up the momentum to get clean, breathable air. We can't live without it."

Population Bomb

World wide, the growth in human population is slowing, but not stopping. Populations are actually dropping in Russia, Japan, and Europe. China has lowered its growth rate by imposing a "one child" policy on couples. Couples are heavily fined if they have more than one child, and women are sometimes forced to undergo abortions or sterilization.

But the population of the world as a whole, and in the United States, is still growing. By 2050, the U.S. will have approximately 100 million more people than it does now. It is expected that there will be 9.15 billion people in the world. (There are almost 7 billion people as of this book's publication.)

Though not all of *The Population Bomb's* dire

predictions have come true, increasing population will put pressure on our ability to feed ourselves. It will strain the limits of available fresh water. It will increase our pollution and impact on the environment. This is already happening in some areas of the world, where there is widespread poverty and famine. We will need to come up with creative ways to solve these pressing problems.

Santa Barbara Oil Spill

After the Santa Barbara oil spill in 1982, a moratorium was placed on offshore drilling on the United States' outer continental shelf. Still the country experienced a major oil spill in 1989, when an oil tanker, the Exxon Valdez, ran aground in Prince William Sound, Alaska.

The moratorium against off-shore drilling lasted for twenty-six years. It was lifted in September 30, 2008 by Congress, with the support of President George W. Bush. On March 31, 2010, President Obama announced that he planned to open large areas of the Atlantic and the Gulf of Mexico to offshore drilling.

On the fortieth anniversary of Earth Day, April 22, 2010, there was an explosion on a BP Deepwater Horizon oil drilling platform in the Gulf of Mexico. The platform caught fire and sunk, killing eleven workers and causing the largest ocean oil spill in history. The Santa Barbara oil spill released an estimated 80 thousand

The BP spill in the Gulf of Mexico, April 22, 2010.

The BP oil spill that occurred on April 22, 2010, caused great damage to the wildlife along the Gulf Coast.

The BP Deepwater Horizon spill

barrels of oil. The BP Deepwater Horizon spill, according to estimates, released 4.4 to 4.9 million barrels of oil.

Once again, visions of oil-coated dying wildlife and tarred beaches flashed across the nation's television screens. As of the printing of this book, the impact on the Gulf's ecology, its fish, birds, mammals, and people, has yet to be determined. America is still driven by its insatiable appetite for oil.

Cuyahoga River

The Cuyahoga River no longer burns. Nor does it smell. You don't have to panic if you fall into it. You can't drink from it yet, but the water is clearer. The Clean Water Act made it illegal to dump hazardous substances in our nation's waters. And the EPA has acted to enforce these regulations and to clean up our rivers.

In the Cuyahoga area, they built better sewage plants. They stopped dumping industrial waste in the river. They also took down the dams, rerouted the river around dams, and built fish ladders to allow free passage for fish and watercraft.

Where once there were no fish, now forty different species thrive. More fish in the river has meant increased populations of birds, and of beaver, fox, and other mammals along the river. There are more fishermen along the Cuyahoga, too. And kayakers and canoeists enjoy the river's beauty.

Many challenges still face our world, such as climate change, depleted fresh water reserves, and the need for renewable energy sources. Rainforests are threatened and species are going extinct at an alarming rate. We need to recycle our wastes and find sustainable ways to feed growing populations. Still the Cuyahoga River is a symbol of what can be done.

Now in America. . .

The Cuyahoga River runs clear. Earth Day is celebrated every year, not just in this country, but around the world. Each Earth Day reminds us that we need to care for the earth that sustains us. Our future depends on it.

In the words of Senator Gaylord Nelson, "Are we able to meet the challenge? Yes. Are we willing? That is the unanswered question."

You can find out more about current Earth Day issues and how you can help at www.earthday.org.

Forty species of fish and other wildlife now thrive in and near the Cuyahoga River.

Earth Day Timeline

1916, January 4	Gaylord Nelson is born in Clear Lake, Wisconsin.
1944, August 29	Denis Hayes is born in Wisconsin Rapids, Wisconsin.
1948, October 26	Smog in Donora, PA kills 20 people.
1962	Rachel Carson publishes *Silent Spring*.
1963	The first Clean Air Act is passed by Congress.
1969	Paul and Anne Ehrlich publish *Population Bomb*.
January 28	There is a major oil spill in Santa Barbara, CA.
June 22	The Cuyahoga River catches on fire.
1970, April 22	The first Earth Day is celebrated.
May 4	The Kent State Massacre occurs. The National Guard opens fire on anti-war demonstrators and kills 4 students of Kent State College.
November	Dennis Hayes helps defeat seven anti-environmental candidates with his "Dirty Dozen" campaign, including powerful congressman, George H. Fallon.
December	Environmental Protection Agency is established by executive order of President Richard Nixon. The Clean Air Act is amended.
1972, June 14	General use of DDT is banned in the U.S.
December	The Clean Water Act is passed.
1973	The Endangered Species Act is passed.
1977	Clean Air Act is amended and strengthened.
1990, April 22	Earth Day goes global.
2001, May 23	The Stockholm Convention is signed by 92 countries, establishing world wide regulations for the use of Persistent Organic Pesticides such as DDT.
2010, April 22	Fortieth Anniversary of Earth Day. There is a major oil spill in the Gulf of Mexico from the Deepwater BP well.

Pins like this one were handed out on the first Earth Day on April 22, 1970.

Gaylord Anton Nelson Timeline

1916, January 4	Born in Clear Lake, Wisconsin.
1939	Graduates from San Jose State College in California.
1942	Receives law degree from University of Wisconsin.
1942–1946	Serves in the US Army as a lieutenant during World War II.
1946	Joins law practice in Madison, Wisconsin.
1947, November 12	Marries Carrie Lee Dotson.
1948–1958	Serves as Wisconsin State Senator.
1953, August 10	His son, Gaylord (Happy) Jr. is born.
1956, June 21	His daughter, Cynthia (Tia) is born.
1959–1962	Serves as Governor of Wisconsin.
1961, May	His son Jeffrey is born.
1963–1981	Serves as United States Senator.
1970, April 22	Founds first Earth Day.
1981	Becomes counselor for the Wilderness Society.
1995, September 29	Awarded Presidential Medal of Freedom.
2003, January 10	Awarded the Olmsted Medal by the American Society of Landscape Architects.
2005, July 3	Dies at age 89 of heart failure. Buried in Clear Lake, Wisconsin.

Denis Hayes Timeline

1944, August 29	Born in Wisconsin Rapids, Wisconsin.
1950	Moves to Camas, Washington.
1962	Graduates high school and attends Clark College.
1964	Earns AA degree.
1964 – 65	Backpacks around the world.
1969	Graduates with B.A. degree from Stanford University.
	Attends Harvard Law School.
1969 – 1970	Organizes the First Earth Day.
1971	Marries Gail Boyer. Becomes visiting scholar at Woodrow Wilson Center at the Smithsonian Institution, studying solar energy.
1972	Enters graduate program in engineering and business at Stanford University.
1974	Directs Illinois State Energy Office.
1975	Is named senior researcher at the *Worldwatch* Institute. Writes book, *Rays of Hope*, on solar energy.
1983 – 88	Runs federal Solar Energy Research Institute during the Carter administration.
1985	Earns J.D. degree from Stanford University School of Law, joins San Francisco law firm.
1990	Runs Earth Day as an international event. Becomes chairman of Green Seal Inc., an organization to develop and promote environmentally sound products.
1993 – present	President and CEO of the Bullitt Foundation which donates money to preserve the environment in the Pacific Northwest.
2000	Organizes Millennium Earth Day.
2010	Helps Organize Earth Day celebrations around the world.

Glossary

Addressograph – (uh DRESS oh graf) A machine that addresses labels.

Amendments – (uh MEND muhntss) Changes made to legal documents or laws.

Appalachian Trail – (ap uh LAY shee uhn TRAYL) A hiking trail in the United States that runs about 2200 miles between Springer Mountain in Georgia and Mount Katahdin in Maine. It passes through the Georgia, North Carolina, Tennessee, Virginia, West Virginia, Maryland, Pennsylvania, New Jersey, New York, Connecticut, Massachusetts, Vermont, New Hampshire, and Maine

Barrio – (BA ree oh) Spanish for "neighborhood." A neighborhood where Spanish is the main spoken language.

Bipartisan – (bye PART UH suhn) Involving cooperation between two political parties.

Civil Disobedience – (SIV il diss uh BEE dee uhnss) Using non-violent means to disobey a government law.

Clear Cut – (KLIHR kuht) To cut down and remove all the trees from a certain area.

Complacent – (kuhm PLAY suhnt) Happy with the way things are; unwilling to cause things to change.

Counterculture – (KOUN tur KUHL chur) A group that is against the way the rest of society lives or behaves.

DDT – (dichlorodiphenyltrichloroethane) The abbreviation for a chemical made to kill insects but which is also poisonous to other animals.

Dysentery – (DI suhn tair ee) A serious disease marked by bloody diarrhea.

Ecology – (ee KOL uh jee) The study of how people and other living things affect the earth.

Entomologist – (en tuh MAWL uh jist) One who studies insects.

EPA – Abbreviation for Environmental Protection Agency. A United States government agency that was created to produce programs that would reduce pollution and protect the environment. Although it was formed by an act of Congress, it is independent.

Establishment – (ess TAB lish muhnt) In this story, the current group that is in control.

Fault – (FAWLT) A large crack in the surface of the earth. Faults are found in areas that often have earthquakes.

Fluoride Gas – (FLAWR ide GASS) A dangerous chemical that can cause serious damage to people's eyes, lungs, and liver depending on how much a person breathes in.

Gross National Product – (GROHSS NASH uh nuhl PROD uhkt) The total value of all the goods that are made in a country for one year.

Heyday – (HEY day) The best time of a person's life.

Hippie – (HIP ee) A movement that began in the United States in the 1960s. Sometimes called the Peace Movement, these young people adopted their own way of living and their own clothing styles.

Lead Arsenate – (LED AR suhn ayt) A chemical used during the late 1800s to kill gypsy moths. Later, plants that had been treated with the chemical were found to produce foods that were toxic to human beings.

Lethargy – (LE thur jee) Drowsiness, laziness, indifference.

Malaria – (muh LAIR ee uh) A disease caused by mosquito bites and usually found in warm tropical areas. The illness causes sweating, chills, and fever.

Mass Transit – (MASS TRAN zit) A travel system used in major cities that uses buses, subways, or trains to carry large groups of people.

Mill Town – (MIL toun) A town that is built near a factory. The factory provides most of the jobs in the town.

Mulch – (MUHLCH) A protective covering of chopped leaves or straw that is spread over a certain portion of ground to help it stay moist and prevent weeds from growing.

Nuclear Test Ban Treaty – (NOO klee ur TEST BAN TREE tee) A treaty that was originally signed by the Soviet Union (Russia), the United Kingdom, and the United States that would stop the testing of nuclear weapons in the air in order to eliminate the problem of "fallout" or radioactive chemicals left in the air by the tests.

Progressive Party – (pruh GRESS iv PAR tee) A political party created when Theodore Roosevelt broke away from the Republican Party. It was also called the Bull Moose Party.

Pyrethrum – (pye REE thruhm) A chemical made from the chrysanthemum flower and used to kill insects.

Right-wing – (RITE WING) Another name for conservative politics. The Republican Party is often referred to as the right-wing or conservative party.

Settlement Money – (SET uhl muhnt MUHN ee) Money paid to settle a legal dispute or law suit.

Teach-ins – (TEECH inz) Meetings organized to discuss a particular topic. The meetings can include lectures and displays and invite those that attend to participate.

Typhus – (TYE fuhss) A disease caused by lice that produces fever, rash, a severe headache, and sometimes confusion.

Woodstock – (WUD stok) A 3-day music festival held in 1969 in northern New York. Half a million concert-goers were entertained by more than 30 musical acts. The event became known as one of the 50 moments that changed Rock and Roll history.

Zero Population Growth – (ZIHR oh POP yuh LAY shuhn GROHTH) Keeping the population number steady by limiting the number of children that can be born so that only enough are born to replace the existing population.

Index

Photo credits

Illustrations credits

Make every day Earth Day.